For all the chicken lovin' children and adults in our world!

Copyright © 2023 Mary Jo Huff
All rights reserved. No part of this publication may be reproduced, stored in a retrieval system or transmitted by any form or by any means, electronic, recording or otherwise without the prior permission in writing from the publisher.

Published 2023 by Storytellin' Time Press

Book design and illustration by Wendy Fedan, Create A Way Design & Publishing
www.CAWpublishing.com

Paperback ISBN: 978-1-959192-03-9

Library of Congress Control Number: 2023902948

Chicken Fun

Written by Mary Jo Huff
Illustrated by Wendy Fedan

Chicken one and chicken two, scratching pecking chomp and chew.

Chicken two and chicken three, scrambling away from the honeybee.

Bakk baba bakkk baba

Chicken four and chicken five, dancing chickens dip and dive.

Bakk baba bakkk baba bakk bakk bakk!

Chicken five and chicken six, laughing at their funny tricks.

baba bakk bakk bakk!

Chickens 1, 2, 3, 4, 5, skedaddling backwards with a jive.

Bakk baba bakkk baba

bakk bakk bakk!

About the Author, Mary Jo Huff

Mary Jo Huff is an author, storyteller and puppeteer creating books for young children. She has worked in 47 states as a teaching artist. Mary Jo is the past director of a center with 115 children, an onsite consultant for Early Childhood Educators, and has written for Frog Street's Pre-K and three-year-old curriculums. She has written for Monday Morning Publishing, SECA, and Gryphon House. Graduating from the University of Southern Indiana and attending thousands of educational training hours Mary Jo shares her enthusiasm and passion for literacy. She lives in a small river town, Newburgh, IN, on the Kentucky border, which gives her writing a twist of southern culture. She and her husband of 60 years have three children, eight grandchildren and 3 great-grandchildren.

About the Illustrator, Wendy Fedan

Wendy's passion for writing and illustration began when she first wrote and shared her stories in the 2nd grade. She is a freelance illustrator and product designer living in Amherst, Ohio. With 25+ years in the design field, she worked for 10+ years at American Greetings as a
Product Designer and then as an Artist for Blue Frog Gaming. After that she's concentrated on growing her freelance business as an illustrator and designer.
Wendy has self-published several books and is a huge proponent for indie publishing. She just launched her own publishing/book shepherding biz called Create A Way Design & Publishing, LLC.

Made in the USA
Middletown, DE
30 December 2024